I'M STARTING WORK

*A practical **guide to
success** in your **first
professional services** job*

I'M STARTING WORK

A practical *guide to success* in your *first professional services* job

By Sue Willcock

MBA Construction & Real Estate, Dip Proj Man (RICS)
NLP Certified Practitioner

Published by Chaseville Press

First Edition: July 2018

ISBN 978-0-9935247-1-4

DEDICATION

To my nieces and nephews who teach me so much about the Millennial generation and inspire me to keep learning.

Sue Willcock

CONTENTS

Acknowledgements ix

Foreword xi

Preface...xv

1. Get off to a good start 1

2. What makes you 'professional'? 11

3. First impressions 19

4. Looking the part 29

5. What is expected of you?............................... 35

6. Continuing to learn 49

7. Owning your career... 59

8. Thinking about your objectives...................... 65

9. Understanding outcomes............................... 75

10. Getting briefed well 83

11. Asking for feedback.. 89

12. Why and how to build your network 95

13. Final reflections.. 107

About the author.. 111

References & further reading 112

Sue Willcock

ACKNOWLEDGEMENTS

Thanks to everyone who commented, fed back and added their own professional experience to this book to help our future professionals get ahead. To Amanda Clack, Director at CBRE and past President of the RICS, to Shyam Visavaydia, Founder of Graduate Surveyors and Daniel Fazal, Assistant Surveyor at GVA.

Sue Willcock

FOREWORD

The aim of this book is to provide a no-nonsense guide for those beginning their career in professional services. It's not about technical competence, but the softer side of success – behaviours, attitudes, networking, being professional, and continual learning.

What is interesting is that this is exactly the sort of 'soft skills' instrument that employers and professionals were already recognising as being needed when we wrote the Royal Institution of Chartered Surveyors (RICS) Futures Report in 2014.

I believe, with an ever-increasing need to tackle the war for talent through diversity and inclusion, that this book provides a practical guide for those entering the professions, in an unadulterated format, and asks and presents the answers to the questions many are afraid to ask. These questions and many more are unashamedly addressed here.

Technical competence is one thing, delivered through professional competence, but often there is a gap in soft skills development to really help drive and support those in their early career. Well, that is exactly the gap this book seeks to fill, and I love it for that.

Many, either through apprenticeship programmes or in tackling inclusivity in particular, have commented on the need for the basics to be explained, particularly to help those that have maybe never had a member of their family go to work in a suit before, or attend a black-tie event. This book helps fill these knowledge gaps.

An investment in the suit you probably can't afford is not a frivolous expense, but an investment in yourself and your career, alongside things as simple as turning up on time – early but never late!

These are the simple rules of professional life, so if you have little or no experience of the reality of working in a professional services business, this book will help you settle in fast and understand what is important to your peers, your managers and, most importantly, to your career.

Sue openly talks as someone who comes from a family background where no one had previously worked in this environment. She draws on her own stories of having to learn to network and develop a learning habit. She even covers how to make black tie events less intimidating as she recalls the fear when she was first faced with a confusing array of cutlery.

Sue talks at length about the behaviours and attitudes that will serve you well. She does this with humour and practicality, and the book gives real-life examples, from a career spanning almost 30 years, of the things you can explore and take on to make your career fly.

I've known the author for over 20 years when, indeed, our own careers were still developing. Now we both champion the need to help and support those entering the professions through our work and extra-curricular activities.

Sue is passionate about sharing her experience and knowledge to help others develop. I love that this book is written at a very human and inclusive level for new entrants, although I bet some veterans will enjoy it too, despite wishing they probably had it in their library earlier in their careers!

Amanda Clack MSc BSC PPRICS FRICS FICE FAPM FRSA CCMI FIC CMC Affiliate ICAEW

Executive Director and Head of Strategic Consulting, CBRE

Immediate Past President of the RICS

PREFACE

So, here you are. You've come through what, at times, may have felt like a rollercoaster ride of exams and tests, and after years of studying, have bagged yourself your first job in professional services. Whether you are training to be a solicitor, surveyor, IT professional, accountant or similar 'professional' role, the chances are you've already done a fair bit of studying to get your first 'proper' job. In today's competitive market, this is no insignificant feat, so let's first take a moment to say 'well done', celebrate at bit and revel in your success. You've already done well to secure paid employment in your chosen profession. Congratulations! And I really mean that. After almost 30 years in professional services, I still remember the excitement at getting the news that I had been offered my first role. It's a big thing.

Now, the world beyond studying begins. All that work you've done, with probably a vague idea of what it will really be like, will start to come to fruition. Real clients, whether they are 'internal', within the organisation you are joining, or 'external' fee-paying ones, will call on your professional opinion. You'll have a line manager who will give you things to do, some of which may be interesting and exciting. But some of it may be hard, ill-explained, or downright dull. There will probably be a team you'll need to get on with (even though you may find some of them supremely irritating at times) and, if my own experience is anything to go by, there will be times when some of the work you are asked to do simply petrifies you or even causes you to question your career choice!

I'm imagining, however, that if you are reading this, you want to succeed. Although of course, if your parents bought this book for you, then maybe it's their wish for you to do well…I'll hope for the former. Or at the very least, that you share your parents' aspirations for your career and success in your first job.

So, this book is written for you. It is based on my own experience in professional services – a sector I know, love and have worked in for a long time. I have literally and metaphorically grown up in the sector. I've worked in public and private sector environments. I've been the trainee asking how many sugars everyone wanted in their tea whilst taking bad notes in meetings (largely because I had no clue what people were talking about – all those corporate acronyms…!), cut my teeth working alongside more senior professionals and then became a middle manager, a Director of my own business and a Partner in a top 5 UK consultancy. I also have over 10 years' experience in developing people in the sector – managers in particular – having designed development programmes for future leaders and managers, designed work experience programmes for aspiring graduates and supported professionals like you, as they strive to become more successful and effective at work.

This book has been borne from a desire to make your transition into the world of work as easy as possible. It's not about your technical knowledge or competence. Predominantly, we'll be looking at the skills and behaviours that it's useful to have as you transition into the workplace and that will help you be successful. My first book, *Help! I'm a manager – A practical guide to success as a first time people manager in professional services* was based on a desire to simply make the reader's life easier, condensing my experience at work into one handy 'back pocket' easy read. It's now a best-selling HR book on Amazon Kindle.

My aim in this book is to maintain a no-nonsense approach by assuming that you are (by the nature of where you've already got to) perfectly able to take concepts and ideas, and apply them quickly to see if they work for you in your own work environment. I've arranged this book so that you can pick out the bits that apply to you, then adapt and tailor them to suit your personality and the specific culture of the organisation you work in.

In the pages that follow, we'll be looking at the importance of building networks, developing your impact and presence, understanding what your boss and your clients really want, standing out for the right reason, cultivating a positive attitude and acting on feedback and other 'non-technical' aspects of your first role.

If by now you are thinking, 'but I'm seriously the best (insert your profession) anyone has ever met so I'm sure not to need this soft and fluffy stuff', then I urge you to stop and reflect for a moment. The Performance, Image, Exposure (PIE) model developed by author

Harvey Coleman and presented in his book *Empowering Yourself – The Organisational Game Revealed* suggests that our success at work depends on our Performance (10%), Image (30%) and Exposure (60%).

This is a depressing model to ponder but, time and time again, I have seen my own evidence of this. When I speak at events, I see plenty of experienced 40-somethings give a wry smile as they consider the reality that this model paints, recalling the people that have progressed in their organisations. Ignore the PIE model at your peril – it is not just what you do that counts at work; it's the way that you do it. And this is where all this other 'fluffy' stuff really, really matters. Trust me.

I've tried to break down the sections in this book into logical action areas so that they are easy to implement. But do bear in mind as you read, that all these areas work together. All of these ideas will help you grow into your role and become the successful professional you wish to be. I wish you luck on your journey.

Sue Willcock

1. GET OFF TO A GOOD START

This chapter is all about some really basic things that are super easy to do but will get you off to a good start in the world of work. The things that, well, I'm just going to tell you in case no one else already has.

For some readers the points outlined here may seem to be stating the obvious, but from conversations I've had with young people just about to start work as they end their college courses or leave university, I know that it's the basics that often catch newcomers out. They find themselves with furrowed brow wondering why they have to do something or wishing they had been better prepared.

Here are a few early pointers, so you know what to expect from the start.

Timesheets

Whilst some modern management theorists suggest timesheets are not the best way to measure effectiveness and productivity, they are still a favourite way of recording time in professional services firms. A timesheet is simply a record of the time you've spent doing the various bits of your job. Different businesses will have different formats and they may be undertaken in a simple stand alone document or via an online system. Essentially, timesheets enable the business to record how much it costs to do different tasks. The information will be put together with other people's timesheets to see how much, for example, a whole project, or a specific activity, costs. Most businesses will ask you to fill in a timesheet showing your activity to the nearest 30 minutes or perhaps an hour and to allocate a code against it. For example, a timesheet might capture information that tells the organisation that you worked on Project X for three hours and whilst on that project did 1 hour of administration and 2 hours of client meetings. Some businesses (like law firms) often ask staff to record their time to the nearest 6 mins. If you have joined a business where the client is charged for the time they spend with a professional, then the timesheet will be used to calculate how much the client pays the organisation. The timesheets in many organisations will be used to work out things like profit (i.e. how much a customer or client pays, less how much it cost to provide it.) so your timesheet, along with your salary will help tell people at work how much an activity has cost (along with other expenditure such as the rent on the office, paper, running the photocopier…etc.). Some firms will be more strict than others on the need for you to fill in a timesheet and will have different protocols for dealing with the information they collect and analyse. My tip though, is that if you are asked to do a timesheet, then simply do it by the deadline required. It's an easy thing to get right and, despite what colleagues might say ('they are boring', 'no one looks at them'…) filling in your timesheets correctly shows that you are off to a good start in doing what's needed of you.

Know your National Insurance Number

If you are based in the UK, your National Insurance number is unique to you and remains the same throughout your life. It is issued by the Department for Work and Pensions and HM Revenue & Customs (HMRC) and is used to help work out what you get paid as well as which deductions have been taken from your salary. These deductions, which are compulsory in the UK (and indeed in many countries, but under different names) are National Insurance Contributions and Tax. You will have been sent an NI number aged 16 and should keep it in a safe place so you have it on hand when you start work. It should appear on your salary slips when they are issued to you.

Bank accounts – know your numbers

You may well already have a bank account. If not, you will very likely need one in your name, so you can be paid your salary at the intervals set by your employer (typically weekly or monthly) directly into your account. Any expenses will also be paid directly into your account. If you need to set one up, you should do so straight away by going online and choosing one that meets your needs. You may be more comfortable visiting a branch and that's fine. The purpose of this book is not to give you financial advice, but please do your own research as to which account suits you – things to look for are the interest rate, any charges, benefits you may get, online banking and cards offered etc. There are plenty of money expert and comparison websites that will give you a view on the best accounts. You will be asked to provide bank details either before you join a firm, or very shortly after. The details your company will need are:

- **The name of the account** (if you are called Fred Smith usually, but your account is in your birth name of Frederick Bartholemew-Farquar-Smith then your employer needs the name your account is actually in!)

- **The Sort Code** This is the 6 digit number that looks like this 12-34-56

- **The Account Number** Usually an 8-11 digit number with no spaces, e.g. 12345678

These details are usually found on the letter you first received about opening your account or on your online banking service, once you have logged in. Never give your PIN number to anyone at work – they do not need it.

Still on money...

You may well be extremely excited to receive your first full-time salary into your own account. Indeed, it may be the first time you've had a 3- or even 4-figure amount hit your account where previously there were only 10s or 100s. You may have looked at the attractive job salary and thought, 'Seriously, I am now loaded!'. BUT, please beware. (And I warn you, this is fairly boring, but I am going to say it anyway.) A few things happen to your salary once you are earning. Let's say, for example, you have a salary of £24,000 a year. I've plucked this from the air as it's easy to do the maths. 'Great', you think. 'That's 24,000 divided by 12 months so I'll be taking home £2,000 per month.' Well, er, no. At the time of writing, you'd be more likely to be taking home £1,630 once tax and National Insurance have been deducted. Ignoring any costs you may have to pay for a roof over your head either living with parents or via rent or a mortgage, you may choose to pay into a pension which is a further deduction. Recently, the UK government insisted we are all 'auto-enrolled' into a pension, so this too will be deducted unless you 'opt out' and say you do not want to pay into a pension.

And just a bit more on money...

Finally, before we get past this topic, a final word on money. Please take it seriously and make it your mission to manage your money well. I cannot give you financial advice, but would urge you to take a look at books and websites that will help you to understand how money 'works'. My first boss once told me to start my pension immediately (I was 18) and, whilst I really had no clue what he was on about (thinking that pensions were just for old people), I signed the forms he gave me. I have never regretted that decision, despite it meaning I took home less money each month as your pension is deducted before you get paid into your account. Think not just about today but the future too. With hindsight, the things I would be looking to learn if I was starting over are:

- How to create a savings habit. Many 'success gurus' ask the question, 'why do we work hard for our money, then give it all to other people, the landlord, the retailers?...' and they advise 'paying yourself first' – i.e. putting money aside. This is a mindset that can seriously change your future, so explore it carefully and guard against simply thinking 'Yay, I've got X to spend...I'm off down the shops'.

- What 'compound interest' is and why people say it's the 8th Wonder of the World... (basically it means you get interest on your interest on your account which, if you only ever have a current account might only amount to 4p a year…but there are so many more opportunities to do more! Well worth looking up.)

- The pros and cons of setting up a pension right now.

- How to manage what debt you may have already (e.g. student loan).

- How much having a job will actually cost you – for clothes, travel and lunches etc.

You would be wise to seek out information on trusted websites such as Martin Lewis' Money Saving Expert, books by Alvin Hall and, early on in your career, get advice from either your bank (where the advice will be based on their products alone) or an Independent Financial Advisor (IFA). Your workplace may run their pension via a specific IFA who may be provided at your workplace.

'Preparation prevents poor performance'

This is an old tip passed on to me by my lecturer at college. Before you start work, do a dummy run of the journey to and from the office at the *actual times* you will be travelling (e.g. peak travel). Not only does this double check your timings, it also takes away some stress from starting on your first day as you know exactly what you are doing and where you are going. Buying train tickets, working out a timetable and dealing with change (e.g. if suddenly your route has to change due to unforeseen circumstances such as a traffic accident or train delays) are key life skills that you will need if you are not confident with these things already. I also did this for my Chartered Surveyor final professional exams which were held in a hotel in London that I had never been to. I made the journey ahead of the day and even went into the hotel so I knew exactly where I needed to go. It definitely takes some element of stress out of the process.

Coffee Break Highlights

- If your firm needs you to fill in reporting tools such as timesheets, do so on time and to the best of your ability. They may feel pointless, but they are important and help managers run the business.

- Consider money matters. Before you spend all your hard-earned cash by giving it to other people (your landlord, any debtors, shops, pubs, restaurants etc.) you would be wise to learn more about financial affairs.

- Help yourself to be on time and unflustered on Day 1 by doing a trial run of the journey at peak times so you know what to expect.

2. WHAT MAKES YOU 'PROFESSIONAL'?

As you may have guessed, I love working in professional services. It's why I write books about our sector. There's just something that makes me feel at home, having begun my early career as a trainee surveyor a long time ago.

So long ago in fact, that there was a certain professional etiquette and hierarchy still in place for us trainees. Some of them just don't make much sense now, or sound downright odd. For example, when I started work in a Local Authority, I was told that trainees were not supposed to speak directly to Partners of the firms we worked with. So, if we had a question for a Partner, our managers had to call them. We always made the tea for meetings (like it was our actual job), did a lot of note taking, typing up, faxing, checking calculations and reading over…Ahh, the heady days of 1980s trainee surveyors!

Alongside my day job, which was focused on learning all aspects of Quantity Surveying, I was also helped and provided with guidance on how to behave 'appropriately' – not just to technically pass my exams, but also abide by the Code of Conduct set by my professional institution (in my case the Royal Institution of Chartered Surveyors) and to, well, 'be professional'.

Today, in a management context, I often come across organisations with a set of 'business values and behaviours' neatly written down – often over many pages with diagrams and frameworks of 'desired behaviours'. Often they include 'professionalism' and, intertwined with this, 'integrity' and 'respect'. But these can be complicated beasts of documents, the likes of which did not exist when our professions first became prevalent. During my trainee journey, I was simply guided and told how I was expected to behave by my managers and peers, and, perhaps more critically, I was shown how to behave through real-life examples of what we would now label as 'role model behaviours'. This was shown not just by managers and leaders, but peers and colleagues – professionals who set a benchmark to follow.

I'll talk more of behaviours later in this book, but for now, here's what I believe makes those of us working in professional services 'professional'.

Whichever professional membership body you aspire to belong to, I would suggest these model behaviours are embodied in your Rules of Conduct, so I would recommend getting a copy if you've not already got one and spending some time really thinking about what these mean for you in your career and in your chosen firm.

As someone who comes from a family where no one had been in professional services before me, lots of office etiquette was new to me as I entered the world of work at 18. And, as my career has developed, I have come to evaluate what being professional means on a daily basis.

Indeed, there were many memorable moments that influenced me, where I really saw this in action through others: a surveyor who left a Practice because he did not like the way things were done, an engineer standing up for what he believed in the face of 15 other people disagreeing in a project meeting, and a project manager calling a dramatic halt to a meeting so that more information could be found to get to the 'right' answer for the client, even though an 'OK' answer was already tabled and we were all in a hurry to move on.

I discovered just how important the values of professional services are to me when I got extremely agitated over some assessment centre candidates having an argument over 'doing the right thing' vs 'making money' in a role play moral dilemma. And, at an event with some school leavers, I had a fantastic debate with one team about professionalism when they sabotaged another team's efforts (albeit in a friendly way) so they could win one of the challenges. I asked, 'Was that professional?', 'Does a client want you to win at all costs?' and, above all, 'Is that acceptable?'

So, here goes – these are my thoughts on six areas that encompass many of the things that the word 'professional' means to me. As you enter the workplace, you should know that it is these things, alongside your technical capability that will make all the difference to your career success:

- **Doing what we say we will do.** That includes being on time and meeting deadlines. Often this means saying no in the first place and not over-promising.

- **Acting in the interests of our clients.** Even when faced with adversity or disagreement from peers or colleagues.

- **Having integrity.** This is an often overused word but for me is about being prepared to take a stand to do what's right.

- **It's OK to say 'I don't know but I will find out' to a client.** Better to be professional than to give the wrong advice because you could not remember something from university!

- **Respecting others.** An easy one – to treat others as we would like to be treated.

- **Dress appropriately.** I often ponder dress in the context of professionalism, especially as many writers say the days of the business suit are numbered (and already gone in many business sectors), and I personally find the idea that a posh pen makes me more credible a hard one to swallow (though I do actually own one). However, I was once told by a personal impact expert that she saw dress/appearance as an expression of respect for the other person. And clearly, it can help engender trust in you as an expert.

This is worth considering in the context of 'looking the part' as appropriate to your role, your environment, and your clients.

As you enter the workplace, think about your intent around your own behaviours. How do you play them out and demonstrate them to others? I strongly believe that it does not matter whether you are junior or a senior member of the firm – we are all on a level field when it comes to the ability to be professional.

Coffee Break Highlights

- You do not have to be experienced to be professional.

- Professionalism can mean many things – respect, integrity, doing the right thing. Watch for role models and see if you can spot good behaviours you would want to mimic.

- Your professional body is highly likely to have a Code of Conduct which you are duty bound to adhere to. It may cover specifics like dealing with client funds or the receipt of gifts at work (beyond the Bribery Act). Make sure you know the relevant Code and adhere to it.

Sue Willcock

3. FIRST IMPRESSIONS

Whichever type of business you have joined, and however 'nice' you think the people who interviewed you are, the hard fact is that you will be being watched closely in your first weeks and months in the job. Whatever your salary or job title, you are an investment for the company and they will expect a return on their investment.

This might sound harsh, but it is the commercial reality – they are paying you to do a job and (whilst they may be expecting you to learn new things and perhaps take longer to do something first time as it is new to you) you are there to get on with the work in hand.

Now, this does not mean that it's going to be like a Dickensian scene from *A Christmas Carol* and your line manager will be a Scrooge-type character ordering you to do this and that, with no lunch or breaks (for a start, there are laws against this!), but there is a baseline against which you are expected to perform. We'll go on to cover how to find out what is expected of you later but for now, here's my list of a minimum level of behaviours that I would expect. I mention these here because I've seen very capable first-job candidates fall down on these issues as they have not made a behavioural transition from school to the workplace. It may sound a bit old-fashioned, but let's be clear – work is not school, college or university. There are different requirements and expectations around how you behave, what is acceptable and what is the norm. What may have been OK or have little consequence in educational establishments could have enormous repercussions at work in an office.

Depending on the attitude that you've had to reach this point so far, the words 'mature' and 'conscientious' may suddenly have to take on a lot more meaning in your life than ever before. When running work experience programmes and working with Graduates at assessment and development centres, I can say that if you put a keen hard worker in front of me who was perhaps technically not as good as a candidate who arrived late with an air of nonchalance that gave me the impression that they were not bothered about work or doing a good job, I'd pick the candidate with the better attitude to give the most exciting work to, or perhaps would pick them to come to a client meeting with me, over the laid back person who may not make such a good impression. Your attitude will be key to your success.

This is the reality of human nature which you can use to your advantage to stand out and get opportunities flowing your way. The good news is that it is easy to make a good impression from the start. Here are some basic pointers:

- **Always be on time**. For work in the morning and for any meetings or other things booked into your diary.

- **Take visible notes in meetings and write down instructions** you are given when you are with the person giving them. You might want to add to them afterwards when they have finished talking, too. I cannot stress this enough so will say it again. *Write things down.* Even if you have the super-memory of a very big brainy elephant, writing things down helps you make sure you understand them. Almost as important, it also shows the other person you are listening to what they have said and gives them confidence that you are actually going to do it. It also helps you manage your time and prioritise. A lot of people may use tablets such as an iPad to do this and that fine. My only advice would be to take note of how your brain works best. Mine works best when I make rough notes and can structure them afterwards in my mind. There's no doubt that an App might work., but each time I try to use one, I find I go back to a pen and a bit of thinking on paper to structure my thoughts. Do what works whilst bearing in mind the perception of others. Do they feel you have understood the brief?

- **Do what you say you will do.** If you are asked to do something and have agreed to do it, well, then do it. This sounds easy, but once you get embroiled in long to-do lists, it is easy to let things that you do not want to do (or do not quite understand) slip into the 'I don't think anyone will notice if I don't do this' category. They will notice. I promise you.

- **Listen and show you are listening.** There are different levels of listening. There's the level that involves a cursory nod and a smile, pretending you are listening when you are not really (I bet you can think of plenty of examples where you do this – we all do it!).

Then there's the level when you are just about listening, hearing the words without actually understanding. And at the top level, there's 'proper listening' – this is where you are intently listening, focusing on nothing else (not drifting off thinking about what you are having for tea later) and putting yourself in the speaker's shoes to really grasp what they are saying and what they need. At this level, your mind will be focused on them, not you. And it means that you are listening with a view to really understanding what they are saying. Which leads us to the next point.

- **Ask good questions.** All too often, I see newcomers to the office environment look just too afraid to ask questions. However, learning to ask good questions is so important that I would rate it as one of the most important skills to develop. Never stop asking questions. I've been at work for almost 30 years and still ask questions for clarity, understanding and learning. If you can develop the confidence to ask questions even when no one else wants to ask, this will stand you in good stead. It also means you should not walk away from a briefing conversation asking you to do something without being really clear on what's expected of you.

- **Lose weak words to sound confident.** If you are less than confident in new situations, try to reduce your use of these 'weak words'. Read the following sentences with and without the weak words – you'll instantly see that you can sound more confident by missing out a few of these.

> **Just** 'I'm *just* the new Graduate'

> **Try** 'I'll *try* to have it to you by tonight'

> **Only** 'I'm *only* an assistant'

> **Perhaps** '*Perhaps* we could do this?'

> **Possibly** 'We could *possibly* try.'

> **I am afraid**… 'I am *afraid* that won't work.'

Now is an appropriate point to tell the story of two groups I once worked with as part of a development programme for young people. I call them my meerkats and my giraffes. Both were groups of aspiring young professionals.

As the programme developed, two groups formed:

- **Group 1**: They were keen to learn. They turned up on time every day, took notes and asked some great questions. They were not afraid to laugh at their own mistakes and were prepared to learn from them and try again until they solved a problem. When they were asked to do something, they asked questions for clarity and then worked hard together to resolve challenges. They were a pleasure to work with. My meerkat group – interested and alert.

- **Group 2**: A member of this group interrupted a speaker we had invited in and said: 'I knew that'. Two were late every day with no apology. One rolled their eyes at a speaker. They cheated during an activity. Need I go on? These are my giraffes. Not that I have anything against giraffes, but their heads were so high in the clouds, I'd struggle, despite their obvious intelligence, to confidently send them to a client meeting and feel they would be respectful and professional.

It's really simple. Be a meerkat. Don't be a giraffe.

Coffee Break Highlights

- Remember, work is not an educational establishment. Making a good first impression through your behaviour will get you off to a good start.

- Get the easy stuff right. Take notes when you are being asked to do something. Be on time for meetings. Do what you say you will do.

- Listen. Take notes. Demonstrate that you are listening by asking great questions to build your understanding. Try to master the art of asking questions for clarity.

- Be a meerkat. Don't be a giraffe.

Sue Willcock

4. LOOKING THE PART

Many of us will be uncomfortable with the idea that we are all judged by our appearance, but even if we grudgingly accept that is the case (however wrong we think it might be), we can make our own decisions as to how we respond.

If you work in an office where it is expected that you look very smart, then you will need to buy yourself some clothes that are appropriate. There are many scales of office dress code – from 'anything goes' to 'we expect you to wear a suit for client meetings'. Check to see if your office has one.

There are often articles in the news about whether it's right or wrong to dictate what people wear, and certainly companies cannot do this if it's deemed to be discriminatory in any way. But, this is a fine and tricky line. I'm not about to debate it here – suffice to say that even if there is no written code, there are often unwritten rules that are part of the office culture or the brand. I once worked in an office where my interpretation of 'dress down day' was a bit too 'dress down', and I got taken aside early in my career and was told I was 'a little too scruffy' – very embarrassing! It turned out that 'dress down' simply meant 'be very smart but you don't need to wear a suit!'. I ended up with three styles in my wardrobe – my work suits, my normal weekend clothes and my 'dress down day' outfits that I never wore elsewhere. It was a bit mad, but for many offices, dress really is important. For others, it will not be. You will have to get to know your organisation and try to understand for yourself whether it's important.

Some words of wisdom I was once given on 'dress codes' comes from an image consultant I worked with who, aside from reinforcing the fact that we are judged in the first few minutes of meeting someone by how we look (including our hair, nails, shoes, jewellery etc.) also gave some wise advice.

'Once you know the norm', she said, 'you can then decide if you want to fit in or stand out. If you do want to stand out, the important thing is that you stand out for the right reasons.'

It's worth thinking about. Standing out as the scruffiest person in the office may actually stop you from being invited to meetings or being given opportunities to tag along with your manager to events, or to see clients and be seen.

Look around at your organisation and assess the 'norm'. Then decide if you want to fit in, or stand out for the right reasons. I've worked in firms where even the pen you have or the watch you wear is something people judge you on. Or where even the cuff of your shirt (double cuff with a cufflink was the norm) was assessed. I have had a client say in horror and almost disgust that someone turned up to a meeting with a satchel. In some places, tattoos and piercings will be acceptable. In others, they will be expected to be covered up. Make sure you know the written and unwritten rules for your organisation. If in doubt (and you can do it without looking odd or getting arrested), perhaps consider a pre-start-date drive over to your new office around lunchtime to see what other people are wearing as they pop out for lunch. It could be useful (though frankly really not worth getting arrested for).

A final point is not to be put off or disheartened if you cannot afford to fit in with your peers' clothes when you are starting out. I have met countless now-senior people who bought second-hand suits and charity shop clothes when they were on the first rung of the career ladder. Don't be afraid of buying something of quality that is second hand and simply washing it or paying for it to be dry cleaned before you wear it.

Here's a secret for you – my first interview was undertaken in the only smart outfit I owned, which was originally bought for my cousin's wedding. When I got the job, I literally had no clothes to wear but I was gifted a few from friends. If you are wearing a second-hand outfit or just have a suit and some shirts being washed on rotation, you really won't be the first! And, if you do need to wear a tie, charity shops have plenty. Venture in, get a bargain, and give to charity. Everyone's a winner.

Coffee Break Highlights

- Like it or loathe it, people will judge you on how you look. Decipher what is the cultural norm for your organisation and then make a conscious decision as to how you respond. Will you fit in? Or stand out for the right reasons?

- Don't be disheartened if you cannot afford too many or any smart clothes and feel you need them. Charity shops and good dry cleaners have seen many a young professional through.

- Don't forget the detail – jewellery, pens, watches, bags – they all make up the idea of 'looking the part'. There are plenty of books on personal branding to read if you want to know more.

Sue Willcock

5. WHAT IS EXPECTED OF YOU?

So far, we've covered some general areas of behaviour such as being on time, looking the part appropriate to your office and taking notes to ensure you understand what is needed from you.

We're now going to look at more specific areas to help you know exactly what is expected of you in your role. Here, I'm going to try to go right back to basics to tell you all the things I wish someone had told me when I started working in an office. There will be people in your firm who will have doubtless forgotten what it's like not to know stuff in the office environment.

If some of this seems like I'm stating the obvious, then I make no apology as I have met plenty of people who, having never worked in an office, just don't know this stuff.

Before we start, it's probably useful to give you a bit of context about the idea of having a job. What is a job anyway? Why does your job exist? This may sound a bit fluffy, but bear with me.

Don't make the mistake of thinking you are just at work to do tasks and cross them off a list. Whilst working hard and getting things done are very valuable traits, it takes more than a completed to-do list to get ahead at work.

At a very basic level, all organisations exist to make a difference in some way. For many, this difference is driven by making money or profit for the owners, either by selling goods or a service to a client or customer. For others, it may be driven by a social need – providing homes, running council services, a charitable organisation etc. In the course of providing these goods or services, things need to be done. There are lots of business management books available which explain how business works and there are many different 'business models' out there – these are effectively different ways in which a business is organised to deliver to their customers or to provide a service. It's worth you knowing what business model your organisation uses to serve its clients, make money or add value. Only then will you know where your role fits. The traditional professional services business model generally works as follows:

A firm of solicitors provides advice for clients for which clients pay a fee based on the time the solicitor spends on the work needed. The clients will pay £X per hour for the service they provide. The firm employs solicitors and other members of staff, has some offices and equipment and trains their staff, which costs them £Y. The success of the business relies on the fact that the total £X fees coming into the business is more than the total of £Y going out!

The reason this is important to know is that your role exists within a 'value chain'. This is a management term which explains how an organisation adds value to its customers and was a phrase coined in 1985 by academic and management theorist Michael Porter in relation to creating competitive advantage. By this, we mean that a client might choose one firm over their competition.

Here are some examples of how a professional services firm may add value over and above their competitors. They may have:

- **Leading experts in their field.** They might be specialists in a specific subject, for example, or write for a leading industry magazine. I used to manage a research function in a large organisation and one of the team was an expert in cost data in the construction sector. He was well known and wrote in the industry-leading magazine at the time.

- **Sector expertise that matches the client need.** Whilst many firms lead on service (e.g. they may say 'we are excellent employment lawyers'), clients will often be comforted by the fact that their chosen professional services firm knows their business well – for example, they may choose a firm that says, 'we are excellent employment lawyers who have 10 specialists in the care home sector'. This gives the firm a competitive advantage when bidding for work.

- **Geography.** You may well think that technology has reduced the need for a client to be physically close to their professional consultant. You may well be right, but people still buy people and often a client will choose a provider who knows the local market where it's important to them. Leeds firms might want to work with others in Leeds or in Yorkshire for many reasons – so they can physically meet them, because they understand the local market, or because they want to 'buy local', for example.

- **Size.** It's often a case of 'horses for courses' here. Clients may pick a small company if they feel they will get a more personal service or a better level of service. They may pick a larger one to reduce their risk of a small firm going bust or to have access to a bigger pool of experts if needed. Size can be a source of competitive advantage.

It would be wise to have a think about the firm you have joined and how it adds value to clients. See if you can answer the following questions after 100 days with the firm. If you can, this will stand you in good stead to ask more commercially astute questions as you progress. If you ask good questions, I believe you'll get noticed as being capable beyond the day job too…

1. What do your clients buy from you? (e.g. what expert advice, sector knowledge…)

2. Why do they buy from you over others? (cost (reassuringly expensive, good value, cheap? They like the Managing Partner?

They know your firm is full of local experts? They trust the firm? They can pop in for coffee? They get a speedy response? There will be lots of these and some of the simplest ones can make a big difference. Although I'm from London originally and picked my first accountant there, based on a recommendation, once I had a baby and lived outside London, I changed, because I needed to have a new local accountant that I could get to easily. I chose one in our village where I could drop in receipts, take my sleeping baby in her carrier and have a much-needed coffee and a natter whilst we did the accounts. Not exactly a strategic decision, but it worked!

3. What pain does your firm take away? Do your clients have a legal obligation they need to meet? Do they simply want to outsource something they could do in-house, but it's not worth it? Does your firms' expertise mean they don't have to worry about something (a fear-based decision) or they can serve their own clients better? (a positive, value-adding decision).

Within this context (ideally before you are in role), you should know and understand very clearly what is expected of you and where you fit in the chain of activities that your firm does to add value to clients (often called 'the value chain' – it's worth looking up if you want to know more).

Although I feel like the statement to 'know what is expected' is blindingly obvious, I am a realist – I know there have been times in my own career when I have not really known what was expected of me or when I have not been clear to others.

I've turned up at work, done lots of 'stuff', been 'busy' and rushed around a lot with a notebook and laptop. Back to back meetings. Busy. Busy. Busy.

But, like many of us at different times in our lives, I can be a busy fool. I can always find things to do, for clients, for the business or for my team.

So, let's get one thing out of the way really early. There are no excuses on this one. You must know what is expected of you. Some firms may simply have a job description. Others may measure you on more comprehensive documents and use words like 'technical and behavioural competencies'. These can be weighty tomes, so let's just say you will be measured both on 'what you do and the way you do it'.

Your business may well have frameworks in place to help you know what these are and if so, get hold of the relevant framework early on.

These will be specific to your organisation but as a guide and for use in your conversation with your line manager, here's a simple checklist to get you thinking about the expectations of you as a new employee in professional services. I've kept these short and broad – you are urged to find out what the specific expectations are in your role and convert these into SMART objectives (more of these in chapter 8) with your own line manager.

What you do

- Deliver a quality service to clients.

- Work as part of a team and support others effectively.

- Win new work, by being good at what you do.

- Deliver results on business projects.

- Develop yourself and look to improve all the time.

The way you do it

As well as your actual duties above, try to find out what kinds of behaviours are important in your own organisation. To get you thinking, some of the most useful 'behaviours' which I've observed over the years are:

- Being a role model for good behaviour in the business (e.g. on time for meetings, always say thanks, being polite, looking the part as appropriate to your business, being positive in your outlook.

- Being a brand ambassador. No rubbishing the company, being positive even in the face of change, being a positive influence on others and 'selling' the brand to newcomers.

- Not being a 'mood hoover'.

- Challenging the way things are done in the spirit of genuine improvement.

- Asking for feedback to improve your performance.

- Creating relationships with others that engender trust.

- Leading the way with innovation and new ideas that take the business forward.

As a first step, I'd advise getting out your job description (often abbreviated to your 'J.D.') and having it in the front of your mind during the first few months as your role develops. There may well be some items on it that meant little to nothing when you joined, but as you get to know the business and where your role fits, they will make more sense.

Don't think that this is just because you are new – most of us have taken jobs when the job description says something you vaguely understand but the detail of which needs time in the business to understand properly. Don't tell anyone I said that though – people will deny it if you ask them, too!

Also, I'd seriously guard against the words 'that's not in my job description'. Unless you are being asked to do something immoral, illegal or downright dodgy – remember that 'value chain'.

You'll get noticed for going the extra mile and humility is a great trait. Yes, I've been a Partner and a Director, but here's the list of just some of the less glamourous stuff I've done (and often still do) on the way. These are all genuine, and I know plenty of senior people who have similar stories. I've:

- Wiped around the loo when a client was coming into the office and someone had left it in an inappropriate state.

- Replaced empty loo rolls so many times in my career I've lost count.

- Set up and cleared away many, many coffee stations and made sure there were enough biscuits.

- Sat filing. For days. Seriously days. Both online filing and paper filing.

- Used my weekend to pack stuff up for

archiving when we moved office. I was a Partner at the point. It needed to be done.

- Emptied bins. Wiped tables. Washed cups. Cleaned the coffee machine.

- Cleaned client data on an excel spreadsheet with over 6,000 entries. It took months. And months. Me and a fantastic team did this as part of a big project. Again, it had to be done. The project probably got me my promotion to Associate. Cleaning the data was a big part of the project.

- Travelled to Heathrow Airport in a cab with a folder late in the evening when my boss left behind some important stuff on his way to Asia.

You get the idea. The small stuff REALLY matters. Moreover, your attitude to it matters. Think about how your firm adds value to clients and where this stuff fits in making the firm work.

Never be too proud or arrogant to do it. If you get an early reputation for thinking things are beneath you, it's a hard one to shake.

Coffee Break Highlights

- Know your firm's value chain, how you add value to clients and your role within the business.

- Never be too proud to do a task unless it's immoral, illegal or downright dodgy.

- You will be judged on what you do AND the way you do it. Your behaviour and attitude matters.

Sue Willcock

6. CONTINUING TO LEARN

So far, we've covered what your role is, what is expected of you and some of the behaviours that will stand you in good stead.

At this point, I invite you to take a breath and reflect on the journey you are on. For many of you, you will be on a path of development that is, for the time being at least, set in stone by your professional institution. You may have to keep a diary, or a record of experience, or undertake further exams to become formally qualified.

I undertook all of my professional qualifications part-time (my degree, my post-grad and my surveying professional qualifications to name a few.) I'm now in a different stage of my career, but will never forget the commitment and resilience it takes to get your professional exams and apply your degree to real-life clients. For me, this often meant working late, then getting home and starting my coursework or my professional diary, or preparing for an exam outside work.

Do not underestimate the power of grit,

resilience and goal setting during this time of your life. You will probably already know that there is a lot more to passing exams and getting your qualifications than just 'being clever' or applying your knowledge. In reality, that 'pass' is often a reflection of the times you said no to going out with your mates, struggling through a topic you found difficult, or having to pick yourself up and start again when you did not get things right first time. Please do not fear or shy away from these times. For what it is worth, I truly believe it's these trying times, when you show grit, resilience and the ability to simply keep going, that can make us all. If you fail an exam, you CAN re-take. If you lose your job, you CAN get another. If you are finding something hard, you CAN persevere and get extra help. You can also do some investigations into your personal strengths to understand yourself more and play to your strengths as your career develops. I feel I can say this from a position of experience – if someone had done any kind of personality testing on me at 18, I would never have become a Quantity Surveyor. I am actually not very good at maths and find things I cannot see hard to visualise. This is not so good when you have a 2D drawing in front of you to measure! But, I worked really hard and got a First Class degree, despite actually crying in my Measurement exam. Did I persevere? Yes. Did I show grit? Yes. Did I go on to understand that my strength lies in people, talking, connecting people and making things happen? Yes.

I know plenty of people who have dropped their professional qualification goal as they have been so busy doing their day job. Then, as they progress, life gets in the way – they may have children, get promoted or move away from their technical core so much at work that it's hard to then go back to get their qualifications.

So, at the risk of sounding (a) old fashioned and (b) like your parents, here's my opinion – of course, you can take it or leave it:

- Focus on finishing your professional qualification and 'getting your letters' as a real priority.

- Once you have them, they are yours. Forever. Projects, clients, bosses and jobs will come and go. If you prioritise the day job and the now, you may risk never getting the qualification YOU need to move on and move up.

- People may tell you 'I never got mine and I was OK'. And they may well be. But, my argument would be, it's better to have them than not. I don't use mine anymore (MRICS) but I could choose to do some work to get them back. They are all mine.

- This is a general statement, but often the older you get, the harder it can be to go back to a learning habit. This is not an ageist statement but just a reflection that the practicalities of life often kick in harder as we grow older – having children or older parents to look after makes it even harder time-wise. Get the professional qualifications done and dusted, even if you plan to develop further in your career.

As a new joiner in the organisation, you may well have access to a Graduate programme or dedicated budget. Even if you don't, there are many ways in which you can integrate personal development and learning into your day job alongside the formality of getting your professional qualification. All of these will stand you in good stead to develop a learning attitude that should continue throughout your working life (I give similar advice to new managers in my first book *'Help, I'm a Manager'* too).

- Reflect on your mistakes and ask yourself what you will do to achieve something different next time.

- Actively seek feedback on your performance. A great way of identifying areas to develop yourself and identifying strengths to build on is simply to ask for feedback.

- Get out of your comfort zone. If getting completely out of your comfort zone is too uncomfortable, set yourself a target which builds on an area where you already have strengths, and then use this to structure your planned development. Make sure you set a clearly defined goal so you know when you've reached it too. For example, if you are OK at writing project reports but want to be brilliant, how will you know what 'brilliant' is? (Feedback, benchmarks with others etc). Once you know 'what good looks like', you can then plan how to get there.

- Consider the Performance-Image-Exposure (PIE) model mentioned in the preface.

- Find some learning buddies. What knowledge might you share with someone in return for some knowledge back? How might you create a buddy relationship to support development for you both?

- Use social media. Many sectors use social media much more than others to learn from colleagues outside their immediate networks (the IT sector is one that springs to mind). Online forums can be an invaluable source of learning. Special interest forums on Linked In, together with specific websites for your sector (websites associated with sector magazines usually have good discussion forums) will help keep you up to date. Follow your professional institution on Facebook, Linked In and Twitter.

- Explore iTunes, YouTube and TED Talks for learning. If you haven't discovered these online learning tools, then go exploring right now.

- Discover audio books Audible.com or other such sites are well worth investigating. Especially if you are a professional on the move – audio books can be a great way of learning. I find a combination of audio books, a speaker pillow (yes, it really is a pillow with a built-in speaker) and downloads on my smartphone for the car mean I can often 'read' a book a week.

- Use libraries and other public resources. OK, so Amazon makes it easy to order books for delivery direct to your door, but a visit to the library not only provides a quiet space for thinking but by simply browsing around can spark thoughts and new lines of thinking. The British Library at Euston, London is one of my favourite places and has a fantastic business centre with regular seminars taking place. Likewise, local libraries are also great resources for self-development (and quiet space). Museums also very often have free entry or specific events that are reasonably priced and may be aligned with your learning goals.

- Question your newspaper, radio and TV choices. Challenge your thinking by questioning your reading, viewing and listening habits by changing for a while and tuning in to new things.

- Go to the free exhibitions attached to

conferences. Many of us receive invites to exhibition/conferences where the ticket price is often prohibitive to attending. My advice here is to weigh up the networking opportunities and the exhibition (think about the PIE model), know who the exhibitors are and plan your day in advance to meet and mingle to meet your needs by just attending the free bit. Often you pick up lots of free learning material from exhibitors and gain immense value from the free seminars and networking. Just be clear on your objectives before attending.

- Plants & nature. There is some evidence to suggest that that plants on our desks are beneficial when working – reducing stress and increasing creativity for some. Beyond the office environment, being close to nature can also help you process information, slow down and reflect. You may not feel that you will work better because there is a plant on your desk, but I think we have all had the feeling that we need fresh air, or to get out of the office and see some greenery to help us think. Reflecting is a really important part of the learning process so don't underestimate what getting close to nature can do for you.

All of these things are great ways of learning and are free or low cost. Some might require you to take courage and be bold to step out of your comfort zone. Many of them can be done as part of your professional qualification, or will help it without much additional effort (e.g. reading a decent newspaper), whilst others may need to be given some thought and prioritised.

Coffee Break Highlights

- Lifelong learning is key to success. Seek opportunities to learn at work and outside.

- Ask for feedback and try and get it as soon as you can to an event. For example, after a meeting, ask 'was there anything I could have done differently?'

- Use resources that work for you to broaden your mind and make good use of a variety of them. Free events can be really valuable, and audio books can make a long journey productive. Choose your news sources carefully.

7. OWNING YOUR CAREER

Years ago, I was pondering over a big life decision that I needed to make around my job and where I lived as a result. It was a hard decision – I asked friends their opinion, sought advice from family and, well, anyone who would listen, to be honest. I think even a visiting dog had its ear bent one night (dogs, for the record, are great at listening but are pretty rubbish with answers). Finally, two months of prevarication and procrastination led me to a coffee with a good friend. His words were wise. 'It does not matter how many people you ask; the decision is yours. No one cares as much about your job as you do. They are too busy worrying about their own life.'

At first, I thought this was a bit harsh. People did care about me and my decision would impact on them too. On reflection though, I realised he did not mean that people did not care about me, just that my life was my life. It was my decision to make.

I tell this story because one of my own bugbears is people who want others to take responsibility for their career and I think my friend's words 'no-one cares about your job as much as you do' are harsh but powerful.

Depending on our own personal circumstances, you may be expecting to work in some form for about 40 years or more. Let's say, for 8hrs a day. 330+ days a year for 40 years. That's a lot of hours in our lives.

Why then, do I meet so many managers in our field that tell me that professional, qualified people, most of whom have been to college for years to qualify in their field, come into appraisal/career planning conversations with a blank sheet of paper, waiting to be told what to do with their career, or asking their manager 'what courses do you think I should go on this year?'

Please don't become a 'waiting to be told' person after studying so hard, for so long. Here are a few reasons why I believe that taking responsibility for your own career is so important:

- **Reason 1:** As my wise friend says, 'no one cares as much about your career as you do.' Not even the best manager in the world.

- **Reason 2:** One of the best bits of advice I was ever given was, 'if you want to get on, make yourself as useful as you can to your line manager'. Don't give them work to do. Entering a career conversation (which is about their career!) with a blank sheet of paper, gives them a job!

- **Reason 3:** Advice passed on to me by an experienced Chief Executive Officer (CEO): If you want to be considered for an opportunity you have to have 'first thought status' – i.e. you are the first person someone thinks of when they see or hear of an opportunity. If you are a passenger in a career conversation, how will anyone, let alone your personal advocate (i.e. your line manager) know what sort of opportunities interest you with clients or in your own workplace?

- **Reason 4:** Only you know what really motivates you. Good managers will coach and guide you, and ask good questions to help, but it is not their responsibility to tell you what you want from your work life; it's absolutely your responsibility to have given it thought.

Taking responsibility for your career does not mean you will always get what you want, but aim to be a fish swimming in a direction you feel you have a say in or are at least happy about, not a flailing about fish who is just following a metaphorical shoal and seeing where they end up.

Coffee Break Highlights

- Rise to challenges. Aim to get 'first thought status' for when something needs doing. It will serve you well.

- Simply being useful to your line manager is one way of getting noticed.

- If you have never been lucky enough to have any personality type testing (often called psychometric testing, at work), these things are worth doing – they identify your strengths and weaknesses and can be really valuable in developing and understanding of yourself.

Sue Willcock

8. THINKING ABOUT YOUR OBJECTIVES

Building on the last chapter, countless times, I have sat in front of a new Graduate and asked them, 'so, where do you see your career heading?' Too often, this is met with a blank look or an 'I don't really know'. I always find it mystifying as to why anyone would spend perhaps four years studying, work hard to get a job and then come to a personal/career development meeting wondering where they might head to next. Please don't be one of these.

This is not to say I want someone to come in to a development meeting and arrogantly set down demands about post-Grad courses, costing the business £25k+ to launch their career in a niche service that we've never worked in, but is their personal passion…

No.

But I do want a two-way conversation. A conversation where we talk about the business direction and need, and where their aspirations might match. For a start, this makes it much easier for me as a manager. There is a marker in the sand with you telling me the things you love and want to be involved with. Secondly, it's a more interesting conversation for both parties. And thirdly, I hear the voice of someone who has drive and passion, not a wishy-washy buoy of a person floating on the water, waiting to see which way the wind blows.

In this chapter, I'll give you some information that you otherwise might not see until you reach a management level. It's advice I give to managers about setting their team members some goals. I'll include the content here re-worded for you as a newcomer to the office so that you can have an insight into what good goals look like. Whilst I would very much guard against telling your boss how to do his or her job, you might instead use this as a framework to consider and prepare for your own first goal-setting session. In your business, this might be called an 'objective setting' session or a Personal Development Plan, or be a part of a performance appraisal process (where you are given goals and measured against them during the year).

Find out whether your firm has such a system in place and take a look at the format as early as possible after joining.

Thinking about your own goals:

An easy way to think about setting some meaningful goals is to consider three parts to the conversation: Delivery, Inspiration and Development.

DELIVERY

Firstly, think about what the business might need from you in the coming 6-12 months. What outcomes do you need to deliver? This is a good place to start because it stops you having some kind of fluffy conversation with your manager about 'how things are going'.

If you do not have a full picture, what do you know that is certain? Do you have a project that lasts until a certain time? Have you been asked to do something specific like create a handbook, design a spreadsheet or help someone deliver to their client? What have you been asked to deliver already and what might you be asked to deliver in future? What might you want to deliver? Is there a particular part of the business you are interested in, where you can see a need?

INSPIRATION

What do you want that might inspire you? Do you want to be a technically brilliant expert, get closer to clients, gain experience in a certain sector? What do you want to get from your time at work? Most people come to work to make a difference in some way. A good question to ask yourself is what difference you want to feel you have made when you go home at the end of each day. Money is just not enough to make any of us work hard or smart, so what else do you want? What gets you out of bed in the morning and choose to work for your firm over their competitors? Can you see opportunities at work where you might do more of the things you love?

DEVELOPMENT

The third level is very much all about you and your development. What do you need to do to grow technically and professionally in the organisation? This is not all about spending money on courses.

Yes, external help is often invaluable, but mentoring, buddying and working alongside a more experienced individual, working on a project that covers new ground or adding appropriate responsibility to your role can all be covered by your objectives.

The specifics within the Delivery-Inspiration-Development framework will depend on your capability and interest and during your conversation with your manager. These will have to be tied to the business need, but ideas that may spark some thought as to how they may play out are:

- You may see a challenging project you'd like to work on.

- You may see an opportunity to move to a new sector/client/service line to apply current knowledge in a new way.

- Secondments to other departments.

- Creating a long-term plan to become the business expert on a specialist topic.

- Taking on some more responsibility.

- Leading team meetings.

- Becoming an external speaker or the 'external face' on a topic that will benefit the marketing and sales efforts of the firm.

Finally, a word about SMART objectives. SMART is a well-known acronym used to help set great goals and objectives. It stands for objectives that are:

- Specific (do X, specifically);

- Measurable (enough to know when you have reached the goal);

- Agreed (between you and the other person),

- Realistic (i.e. achievable);

- Time-related (e.g. to a deadline or timescale).

It's a memorable model which is best used alongside the DID framework above, as a way to hone down what actually needs to be done so it can be measured.

Your firm may use a different model but it's worth knowing what a SMART objective looks like as they are great to look back at and know if you have succeeded!

By way of example, think of a discussion with Freda the Graduate, based on the following objectives. How well do you think each meeting would progress if you were New Manager 1 and New Manager 2?

'So, Freda, we are going to review your performance for the last few months. Let's talk about whether you met the goals we agreed.'

New Manager 1 has to base her conversation on these goals:

1. Deliver Project Zebedee.

2. Write the new guidelines for dealing with client complaints.

3. Make sure all invoices go out on time and are paid.

New Manager 2 has to base her conversation on these goals given to Freda:

1. Deliver Project Zebedee in order to yield a 7% profit by the end of the project in 10 months' time. Freda's target is also to win at

least one piece of repeat business with this client over the course of this project and to maintain or exceed the firm's 8/10 customer satisfaction score with this client.

2. Create new guidelines for dealing with client complaints. This should be completed in draft in 2 months' time, allowing time for a review and sign off by the Board. The Guidelines are to be live on the firm's website on 1st March.

3. Prepare and arrange internal sign off of invoices so that they are all issued to clients by the 5th day of each month. Monitor payment of the invoices and provide a report of debtors (detailing reasons for any unpaid invoices) on the 30th of each month for the Board Meeting on the 1st of each month.

Although the latter, SMART objectives can take longer to create and agree, think about how much easier it is to Deliver, Inspire and Develop someone using a SMART objective. It's also easier to monitor these over time so that evaluation is made simpler. Even if your firm does not use SMART, I would urge you to ensure the elements of this system are in your goals as this will help you know what you are aiming for when working on one of your objectives.

Finally, please go into the goal setting meeting with your 'grown-up' head on, remembering all the things about the value chain we talked of in chapter 5. Your firm exists to make a profit and to provide an excellent service. If you want to learn French but you have no clients in France, it's not likely to appear in your work personal development plan. If you want to develop an understanding of some latest regulations and this is a new area of service for your business in helping clients, well, you may well get to be part of the project team.

Coffee Break Highlights

- Own your career. Remember no one cares as much about your career as you do. Aim for a plan, so when an opportunity arises, you can assess it against your plan. Plans can only change if you have one in the first place!

- Think and plan before entering a personal development conversation.

- Remember you want to try and agree goals that cover Delivery, Inspiration and Development (DID) and are also SMART.

9. UNDERSTANDING OUTCOMES

Many years ago, when I was a developing manager, I was told by an experienced leader that I was viewing an issue I was grappling with through the 'wrong end of the telescope'. I had entered the conversation hoping for some specific advice but instead had got an analogy about telescopes. It was not quite what I was looking for.

Later, however, I reflected on his comment as being one of the most useful pieces of advice I've ever been given in my career. What I want to do in this chapter is to let you into the concept of outcome thinking as early as possible in your career, as it may well be a life changer.

The 'outcome approach' invites you to always look at the horizon at the end of the telescope, before commencing with the detail of what you do. In other words, clearly identify the outcome you are trying to achieve before you look at the tasks that make it up. My favourite definition of this approach comes from a group of delegates

I worked with a few years ago.

Taking an outcome approach means…

What you do and the way that you do it should be influenced by the outcome you are trying to achieve.

This transcends everything you do – for clients, for your manager, for yourself. Even at home. When undertaking any task, you need to first understand the ultimate result that you are trying to achieve. Turn your telescope around and see what the outcome is on the horizon.

Most people I know will have given some thought to what they might want to achieve in the coming year – either personally, professionally or both. For many of us though, we might have made plans in the past only for them to gather dust, metaphorically or literally on our desks, perhaps leaving us with a sense of under-achievement or (at the least) a bit demotivated.

This approach helps you to make your plans more meaningful for you, your business and your manager by focusing first on the outcome you are trying to achieve – i.e. the 'why', before moving onto the 'what' and 'how'.

The reasons why this 'outcome approach' works are:

- It focuses on why you are doing something, and in the process filters out 'noise' and 'stuff' that might otherwise distract you;

- It helps make your goals positive – you will be driving towards something, not doing something just to 'fix a problem' or move away from a negative situation;

- The 'what' becomes intensely focused and you can make better decisions;

- You are more likely to be motivated by the 'why' and the results it can give you. These are often more motivational than the practicalities of the 'what';

- You will have a clearer picture of what success looks/feels/sounds like for you so will recognise it when you get there;

- It makes objectives even SMARTer.

So, when planning for maximum effectiveness, try to build an understanding of the business and ask good questions so you can:

1. Understand desired outcomes. What ultimate outcome are you being asked to achieve? Don't be afraid of asking 'what is the client trying to achieve here?', 'What's their intent?' or "What's the most useful outcome?'

2. Only now should you start to consider HOW you might you achieve them. What works now, what could be better? Are there different means to achieving the ultimate end goal?

3. Make a plan with the outcome in mind.

Now get rid of anything in your plan or on your to-do list that does not contribute to your desired outcomes. Get focused.

All too often, people start with the 'how' but time spent on Step 1 is invaluable. Let me give you an example:

As a manager, I might ask Wilma to attend a training course called 'Winning Business'. This, however, is not the outcome (neither is it a

SMART objective). If we were to turn this into an outcome we would use our telescope to look to the future. What is it we are trying to achieve for the future?

It may be:

- Develop and inspire Wilma.

- Win more business.

- Provide Wilma with some CPD hours.

- Turn Wilma into Salesperson Extraordinaire.

As you can see there are a number of outcomes that are all possible from sending Wilma on a course. Suddenly, two things become clear:

Firstly, depending on the outcome you want, the sales training may or may not be worth the business spending time and money on.

Secondly, Wilma's objective can be made more empowering for her (i.e. give her more autonomy over how she does this) and more impactful for the business if it is outcome-driven.

Let's assume the outcome we really want is for Wilma to win more business. Her SMART, outcome-driven objective may now read:

'Generate 5 new fee-paying clients of over £20,000 value each for our team, within the next 12 months.'

The course is now just part of the process to make this happen. Depending on Wilma's level of capability and motivation, you may decide to add a bit more about the 'how' to her objective.

'To support you in this, we will fund your place on the "Winning Business" course in January. You should be prepared to bring back the learning from the course to the team, so they can support you in your goal. You do not have to win all the clients alone but should use the course to make it happen within our team.'

There is only one question you really need to ask in order to start to get used to managing outcomes and that is, 'Why?' Keep asking yourself 'why are we doing this?' until you are happy that you have the right level of outcome.

For a newcomer to the workplace, outcome thinking will be something that stands you in good stead for development and growth as your career progresses and is a skill to be developed alongside your knowledge of how business works. Just this short introduction though should encourage you to ask better questions to understand why you are doing something. Questions like:

- What are we trying to achieve here?

- What's the bigger picture?

- What are the commercial implications of any decision?

- Do we have all the information we need to meet the outcome?

- Can we meet the outcome in a different, more innovative way?

This is the type of thinking that will get you (a) asking good questions (b) making better decisions and (c) most likely noticed as fantastic future talent for the business. (Just remember what we covered in chapter 5 about adding value and competitive advantage...)

Coffee Break Highlights

- Turning your telescope around is a powerful metaphor.

- What you do and the way you do it should always be influenced by the outcome you, your boss or your clients are trying to achieve.

- In your head, keep asking 'why are we doing this?'. Once you get an answer you are happy with, work backwards to understand what you need to get there.

10. GETTING BRIEFED WELL

Remember all those times your lecturers and teachers told you to read the question in an exam paper many times until you know exactly what it's asking? Well, work is not much different except that for the most part, the question is not written down or articulated in a slick well-thought-out way. No, often the question is vague, worded as a task or a 'to-do', with little context or background information. And unlike an exam paper, assumptions can only be used with caution, for in the real world making assumptions can be very dangerous – hence the old phrase 'to assume is to make an **ass** out of **u** and **me**.'

Time is precious in any professional services firm and often the pressure of client work can mean that explaining something new to someone can be frustrating, hurried or done in a way which does not support their learning or getting something done fast – often managers end up just telling you what the answer should be, or badly explaining what's needed, with little context.

Having recently worked with some young people just starting on their journey into a professional services career, here I set out how to get the most from any session when you are asked to do something – make sure you walk away with a clear understanding of what is required. Key points to consider are:

When is the task needed by?

Know precisely what is needed by when. You may well have a deadline that you need to meet and, of course, this should be clear. However, it's also powerful to discuss any mini-deadlines when you can check in mid-way through. This gives you permission to ask questions to see if you are on track. Do this well ahead of the deadline in case you have not quite got it right. Agreeing mini-deadlines and check-in points can also help you to learn to plan ahead.

Ask for context

Context is important as it empowers you to ask intelligent questions. This means you can add more value to the process. This is also an important part of understanding that value chain we talked about in chapter 5. 'I had to check prices all day', 'I had to make sure stuff was filed properly on the system', 'I had to take notes in a meeting' are some of the woes I hear from newcomers who have not realised the context of what they are doing. Asking for context is really easy and makes all the difference as you may then hear things like: 'It's really important we make sure this report is accurate before the bank signs off funding' or 'Your notes will go to the client as an accurate record of the meeting.' Meeting notes can be used in a dispute, so a key skill is to take accurate notes that are clear years down the line.

Follow up meeting notes with a conversation

This can be helpful to make sure any technical phrases or acronyms are explained to you, and can be helpful to you build your learning.

Ask about acronyms you don't know

If I was to ask you to write down all the acronyms your organisation uses on a day to day basis, I would wager that there would be a fair few. From industry jargon to abbreviated client names, you will be met with a barrage of them in business. CAT (short for catastrophe) plans, BUMs (Business Unit Managers, if you were wondering), HOCs, BULs, PMOs, KPIs, POMs – I've worked with them all!! Never be afraid to ask what acronyms mean. 'Paula – we are working for ABC on Project Silver at their HQ in the UAE so please can you call the M&E guys over there and ask them about the BIM platform they are using as we need to brief the QS team in the UK' does not an empowering briefing make. I have overheard these types of conversations and seen the look on poor Paula's face as she walks away not really knowing what she needs to do or why. Indeed, I have been Paula quite a few times in my career. Don't be Paula.

Ask great questions

Asking great questions is a powerful skill, so when you're doing a task, prepare some questions for your manager that may be beyond the immediate task. These will help you understand the context and the outcome – both of which are valuable skills.

Coffee Break Highlights

- Remember what your teachers said about understanding your exam questions before you start writing? Being briefed at work is very similar – always aim to know what you are being asked to do.

- Making assumptions can be very dangerous – hence the old phrase 'to assume is to make an ass out of u and me.'

- Always check your notes, seek to understand acronyms and ask enough questions until you are happy you understand the task.

Sue Willcock

11. ASKING FOR FEEDBACK

You may not like to hear feedback, especially if it is critical of your performance. None of us does. But, the reality is that if someone gives you genuine feedback, it is really useful. It's their perception of your performance and, if you trust their opinion and it's genuinely coming from a place where they want to help you, then listen, and then you can choose to take it or leave it.

Often, it may be that feedback will hurt a little. I know I have had times when I have become very defensive and told myself I am nothing like the person they are describing, only to go home, reflect on it and concede the person may have a point! It's hard to take criticism, but feedback is a great way to grow. Bear in mind that you may need to have some 'hippo time' when your confidence has been knocked. This is a phrase coined in Paul McGee's book, *S.U.M.O., Shut Up Move On* – where you need time alone to wallow in mud like a hippo and reflect.

Before I give you some ways to ask for feedback, it's worth knowing that it's useful to dig deep if someone gives you feedback:

- Feedback has to be specific enough to give you an idea of how you can improve. Ideally, you'll receive it straight away so, for example directly after a meeting, you might want to say, 'did you have any feedback for me on my performance in that meeting. I'd love to know how I could improve.'

- It's useful to understand what the 'observable behaviour' is. What does the other person actually see? For example, someone may say 'you looked shy', whereas it would be more powerful to say, 'you appeared nervous because you did not make eye contact with the client and twiddled your pen whilst talking,' See how much more useful the latter is in terms of improving? Without being confrontational, try to get some specifics so you know what you could change. Recently, I was told I sometimes say, 'Can I just say…' in meetings before I say something. I was told they felt it was a sign of me asking for permission to speak, which they found odd. I'd never really noticed and to be honest thought I was being polite, but it was great feedback to get as it was weakening my impact in meetings. I don't do it any more!

Two models people I've worked with have often found useful are set out below.

Firstly, you can ask:

1. What might I stop, start and continue to do to improve?

2. What went well and what might I do differently next time?

Or you could ask for feedback in the form of 'three stars and a wish'. This is a model I learned from a 9-year-old, so earns its credibility from primary school. I love it for its memorability and simplicity. You simply ask for three good things a 'wish' for something to be different going forward.

Just ask. That's it. Really simple.

Finally, remember to take feedback for what it is. It's just feedback. Remember, you can choose to take it or leave it. Whether you do so will often depend on whether you trust and like the source and believe it. If someone told me I needed to be very serious each and every day to get promoted, I know I could not do it as having fun at work is really important to me. If someone said that I needed to make more notes to ensure I remembered things, I'd probably go home and reflect that that was a good point and something I could and should act on.

Coffee Break Highlights

- Always remember that feedback is designed to be useful and to help you improve.

- Try to get enough information so you can make a change. For example, if someone says, 'you often seem bored' you may ask them what they see or hear that makes them feel this way. Only then can you act to make a positive change.

- Even if the feedback is something you don't like, always reflect on it and then decide if you want to act on it.

Sue Willcock

12.WHY AND HOW TO BUILD YOUR NETWORK

'Networking' may be a word that conjures up a picture of a very dull five-course dinner talking to people you don't know whilst working out the etiquette of which cutlery you use for the fish course. I'll be honest, it can sometimes mean this. But it doesn't have to and increasingly these days it doesn't. What it can mean is:

- Joining relevant work-related groups on social media sites such as Linked In.

- Belonging to specific face-to-face networking groups specific to your areas of interest of development.

- Attending local evening events from your professional institution. Think of those 'Continuing Professional Development' (CPD) hours too!

- Specifically making a link with someone of interest to you via e-mail, Twitter, Linked in or similar.

- Creating an internal network around you in your workplace that helps you develop.

You may be thinking, 'Seriously, I don't have time to network. I work X hours in a week and can't wait to get home, I don't want to do anything else.' This is your choice but before you decide, it's worth considering the following great reasons to build a network outside your organisation:

- You will learn things you may not have learned otherwise. External events often have great speakers, they broaden your outlook and you'll get to hear a view that might be different to that within your business.

- If you get known in a broader network, this will be great for your own development internally in terms of profile, but also might bring you your next career move!

- You will learn the art of talking to anyone and having to make positive conversation about work, your organisation and what you do. This will be easier for some than for others. Many of you will have an natural ability to talk to strangers. Others will need to develop this skill and networking external to your organisation is a good place to learn.

My advice would be to network with purpose. You don't have to be out every evening at your Professional Institution's dinners, but do know about relevant events and do your research before you go so you get the best from it. This means:

- Know what you want to get from the event.

- Look at the guest list if you can before you get there. Who might you want to meet or talk to?

- Do some research before you get there – is there a great question you can ask when you are there?

- You may choose to Tweet or post on social media that you've been (depending on your organisation's policy).

- Check the dress code. If you want to stand out, stand out for the right reasons!

The other element of networking is internal, within your organisation. Building a network of friends, colleagues and mentors is important for a few good reasons:

- Having people that you have built a relationship of trust with can make all the difference when you are having a bad day. Having a friend at work is known to be a factor in being happy at work. It's important.

- Being surrounded by positive people within the organisation who love what they do and are role models for all the good things about the firm makes it really easy for you to know 'what good looks like' when it comes to what's expected of you.

- You will learn from them. If you have a chance to attend networking events in-house or open training events, or even eat lunch with others – embrace it and join in. Meeting others, whatever their role in the organisation, is always an opportunity to learn more about what they do and the firm. How does their role fit with yours? How do they help the business serve its clients? What is their specialist subject?

Making conversation

It's fair to say that even some of the most confident people I know tell me they 'hate networking' and the 'irrelevant small talk' at work-related events. You may be naturally shy, or at times may feel out of your depth with a topic of conversation. Here are a few pointers that might help:

- Don't try to be someone you are not. Be polite and genuine. Smile.

- Practise explaining what you do in one or two sentences. This will help you to confidently say what you do at work if someone asks.

- Ask the other person about themselves and be genuinely interested in the answer.

- Rest assured, those senior people loitering around the coffee table often feel as awkward as you do when they walk in. They've just done it more and had a chance to practise! A good time to break the ice is when you are gathering around on arrival, when there's no pressure to ask about work.

Simply turning to someone and asking if they would like the milk, asking them how far they travelled, or what their journey was like can stem into a conversation that flows into business.

Eating in a 5-star restaurant like you belong there.

Now, you may wonder why I'm including this. You may think this is outdated and irrelevant, or you may have a background where everyone knows already. But, I know that not everyone does. And I didn't either until I learnt. Before I became an Associate and then a Partner, Pizza Express was my restaurant of choice. In fact, it probably still is.

But when you are being interviewed for a role at the Oxo Tower, overlooking the Thames (as I was latterly in my career), or out with a client at a 5-star restaurant, you probably can't be asking for extra dough balls and whether they have a 2-for-1 special on. It's more productive to just feel quietly confident. I can assure you that you won't be alone in having to learn this stuff – I know many leading firms that train new Partners in dining etiquette. And just think of new members who marry into the Royal Family who, if the newspapers are to be believed, receive 'royal training' in etiquette. Just like your technical knowledge, this 'softer stuff' can also be learnt to help you feel more confident. If your career does take you to more senior positions (or even if it does not) the chances are there will be a 'black tie' event somewhere along the way when you work in professional services.

It's worth knowing the layout of formal dining so you don't start by eating someone else's bread roll or drinking someone else's wine! I've been to many formal events and watched as people wait for one confident person to start before they know which roll to eat and which cutlery to use. Especially if there's a fish course with an extra row of knives or two extra forks for a salad or some cake! I've sat in restaurants where we've been brought *amuse bouche* (pronounced 'amooze boosh') and someone has said, 'We did not order that,' without knowing that often five-course meals open with this dish – something that can be eaten in one bite and is designed to prepare the palate for the dinner to come. Then there are palette cleansers – a tiny mouthful that is designed to neutralise your taste buds so that one course's flavour does not influence the next. Often they are little sorbets like melon. I personally don't think anyone should be judged on whether they know how to pronounce *amuse bouche* or *foie gras,* but I know that like most things, if you know what's coming you can be more confident in unfamiliar situations and this then frees up your mind to engage in conversation and enjoy the company. That's why I'm including it here – so you can be forewarned and forearmed if it's an area that makes you nervous.

If you are invited to a meal where you feel you may be intimidated by an array of cutlery, don't be scared of laying a table at home and practising what a five-course meal table setting looks like. The general rule is start from the outside and work inwards when it comes to cutlery. Your bread roll is on your left, as is your napkin. Your glasses for drinks are on your right. A five-course meal can vary from country to country, but in the UK might consist of:

Amuse bouche to prepare the palette.

1. Soup course.

2. *Entrée*. Usually a small portion.

All of the above are designed to build the palette up to the main course.

3. Main course – usually fish or meat.

4. Cheese course to 'close the stomach'.

5. Dessert – from the French *deservir* – to 'clean the table'.

When you know that the idea is to take you on a kind of 'taste journey', a formal table setting does not seem quite so daunting, as what is before you are simply the tools for the job! There are various types of layout which will differ depending on the courses you are having, so take a look online to familiarise yourself with what you might see.

Finally, ordering wine. As your career grows, you may be the person people look at to choose the wine over dinner. I have to say, I've never really cracked this one as I'm not a wine connoisseur and never will be. I am confident enough these days to just say this, and I let someone else order as it's just not an area that interests me. I have friends though who have spent time learning about fine wines because they enjoy it. If you fall into neither of these categories, you can always steal this trick: I have seen two very senior and confident men consistently order the same grape every time. Now, fine wine lovers will cringe at this, as technically you perfectly match the wine to the meal. But I've seen this used as a backup – they know that they need a white wine or a red wine up their sleeve, but they then rely on a particular one every time. They look confidently at the wine list, pretend they are pondering intelligently and then always order the same one! 'Mmm, (the blah blah) Merlot please,' they'll say confidently, like they know their wines. But really, it's because it's the one they know they can rely on. Personally, I prefer not to blag it, but I guess it's all in the delivery!

A final word on networking

I mentioned online forums and networks earlier and my so my final word on networking is about these in particular. Be mindful that people will almost certainly look you up on social media before they meet you. Whether that's for an interview, ahead of a client meeting or even an informal meeting. Know what is public on your social media feeds and think about your posts. Linked In, at the time of writing, is the most prevalent platform for professional services. I would urge you to fill in your profile properly, with a professional looking photograph, your qualifications and, over time, collect some recommendations. Building your network on this forum could lead you to your next career move, help build a highly positive brand or at the least influence it. An inappropriate tweet or Facebook photo could do the opposite. Be mindful when you post.

Coffee Break Highlights

- Building your network can be critical to your career. It's that PIE model again!

- Build a network on Linked In. Be mindful of what is public on your other social media accounts.

- If you are worried about an event, remember that practice makes perfect. If you have to practise for a five-course meal, or introducing yourself to others confidently (or even a good handshake), just do it!

13. FINAL REFLECTIONS

We've reached the final chapter and I sincerely hope that by now you have tried out some of the ideas in the book and had success with some of the things I've spoken of. In closing, I wanted to give you some final pointers to help you. They are all simply personal reflections on attributes I believe will serve you well on your career journey. They are nothing to do with capability, but all to do with attitude and mindset. If you've read any books on 'success', many of them refer to the difference between success and failure being poised on a razor edge – meaning that a tiny habit or behaviour can make all the difference to which side you end up on. Here are my own reflections on the behaviours that make a positive difference. It does not mean I've cracked them all, by the way, but I've seen them make a difference when I, or others, do!

Planning

From planning long term goals and planning your career development, to making to do lists. Things may not go to plan, but by having plans, you have a starting point and some guide rails in your mind that then lead to goals and a sense of focus. Planning, goal-setting and focus are all behaviours that commonly lead to successful outcomes. Focus means that you'll say no to stuff outside the plan. Even if this means saying no to going out on a Friday night because you want to get a course finished so that you can progress.

Responsibility and ownership

Please have your own plan. Take responsibility for it. Of course, you are getting paid to do a great job and you should do it to your best ability. But, please carve and influence your own path too. Work hard to get what you want and have your own mind. If you've always wanted to work in a certain sector or area of expertise in your field, try and influence that. Don't be a buoy floating out in any direction just dictated by your workplace. Own your career. You can do this through courses, networking and having the right conversations with your line manager.

Perseverance

I can't stress this enough. As I look back on my

career and some of the challenges I have right now, perseverance serves me well on all levels. Stick at things. Even when they get difficult. From a report that you are struggling with, to a long-term goal that's really important to you, working out techniques that work for your personality and mean you stick at things WILL make a difference. For me, these include taking a walk in the middle of a tough mental challenge, often closing my eyes, taking a deep breath and starting over, admitting mistakes and trying to do better next time, stewing on a problem overnight and then making a conscious decision to move on. Choosing to listen to or ignore feedback (we always have this choice!). Giving up things I like to make other things happen. This book, for example, has been written amongst a full-time job and being mum to a six year old. Let's just say, there have been many late nights and not much television or social media in the last year! I've also had to stop doing other personal projects that I also had running alongside, in order to get this one over the line. In many businesses, people who finish things can be rare and therefore prized. Lots of us like 'shiny new objects' and new ideas but run out of steam when it comes to getting things finished.

So, to end, I'll leave you with one of my favourite quotes of the moment from success guru, Bob Proctor: 'Be like a postage stamp – stick to it, until you get there.'

You've worked hard to get into professional services. You've landed a job, and there's a whole world out there for you to explore, grow and develop within, alongside applying and developing your professional knowledge. Whatever background you come from, it's where you are heading and the difference you make to others and the world that will count.

Remember, there is only one you. Now is the time to spread your wings and go and make a difference. Enjoy the journey!

ABOUT THE AUTHOR

Sue Willcock is the author of *Help! I'm a manager – A practical guide to success as a first time people manager in professional services* – a #1 Amazon Kindle Bestseller. She has worked in the sector for almost 30 years, having started her career as a trainee Quantity Surveyor, going on to be MRICS qualified and then moving into a career in leadership development within the sector. She currently holds a change management role within a professional services firm.

REFERENCES & FURTHER READING

This book represents the culmination of my own experience and the influence of significant books that have made a real difference to my thinking and approach. Here's a list of a few of my favourite books which have influenced my thinking and developed me as an individual and a manager which you may find of value.

Empowering Yourself – The Organisational Game Revealed, Harvey J Coleman ISBN-10: 1449080340 ISBN-13: 978-1449080341 (Includes the PIE model)

Managing the Professional Services Firm, David Maister, ISBN-10: 0743231562 ISBN-13: 978-0743231565

How to Win Friends and Influence People, Dale Carnegie, ISBN-10: 0091906814, ISBN-13: 978-0091906818

Eat That Frog – Get More of the Important Things Done Today, Brian Tracy. ISBN-10: 1444765426, ISBN-13: 978-1444765427

Drive – The Surprising Truth about What Motivates Us, Daniel Pink, ISBN-10: 184767769X, ISBN-13: 978-184767769

Start with Why – How Great Leaders Inspire Everyone to Take Action, Simon Sinek, ISBN-10: 0241958229, ISBN-13: 978-0241958223

The First 90 Days – Critical Success Factors for New Leaders at All Levels, Michael Watkins, ISBN-10: 1422188612, ISBN-13: 978-1422188613

The 7 Habits of Highly Effective People, Powerful Lessons in Personal Change, ISBN-10: 0684858398, ISBN-13: 978-0684858395

S.U.M.O. (Shut Up, Move One), The Straight-Talking Guide To Succeeding In Life, Paul McGee, ISBN-10: 0857086227, ISBN-13: 978-0857086228

Sue Willcock

Printed in Great Britain
by Amazon